The Baking Book

Jane Bull

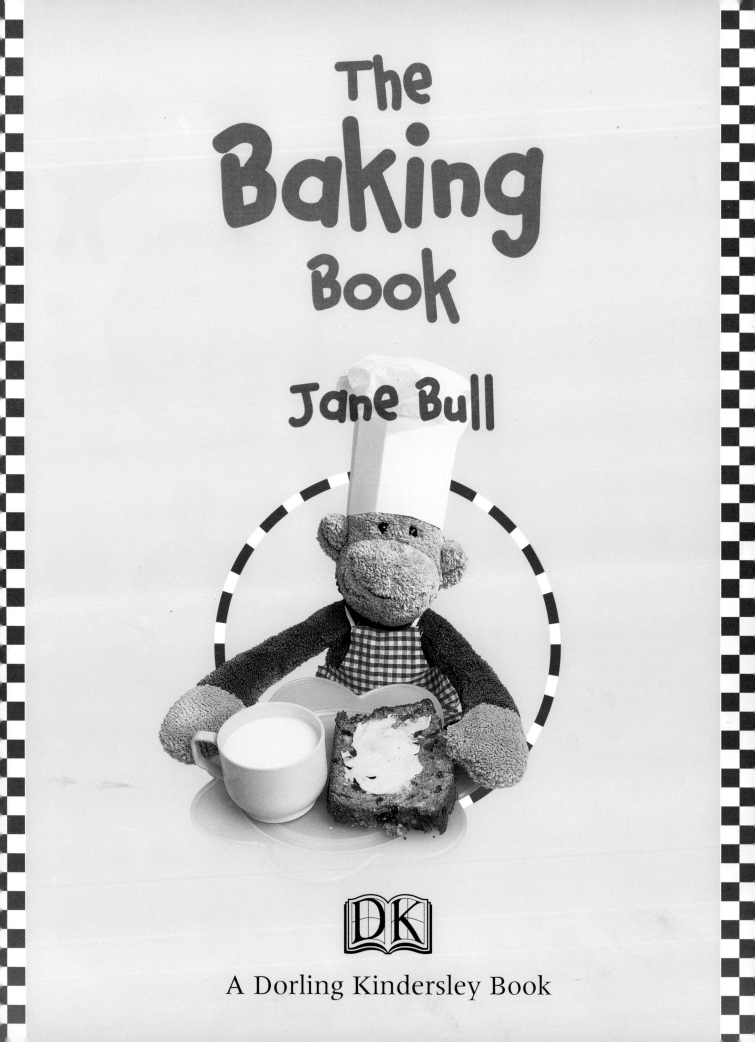

DK

A Dorling Kindersley Book

LONDON, NEW YORK, MUNICH,
MELBOURNE, and DELHI

DESIGN • Jane Bull
EDITOR • Penelope Arlon
PHOTOGRAPHY • Andy Crawford
DESIGNER • Sadie Thomas
DTP DESIGNER • Almudena Díaz
PRODUCTION • Alison Lenane

PUBLISHING MANAGER • Sue Leonard
MANAGING ART EDITOR • Clare Shedden

For Baba

First published in Great Britain in 2005 by
Dorling Kindersley Limited
80 Strand, London WC2R 0RL

A Penguin Company

2 4 6 8 10 9 7 5 3 1

A CIP catalogue record for this book
is available from the British Library

ISBN: 1-4053-0667-X

Colour reproduction by
GRB Editrice S.r.l., Verona, Italy
Printed and bound in Italy by L.E.G.O.

Discover more at
www.dk.com

Bring out the chunky cookies

Bake a batch of . . .

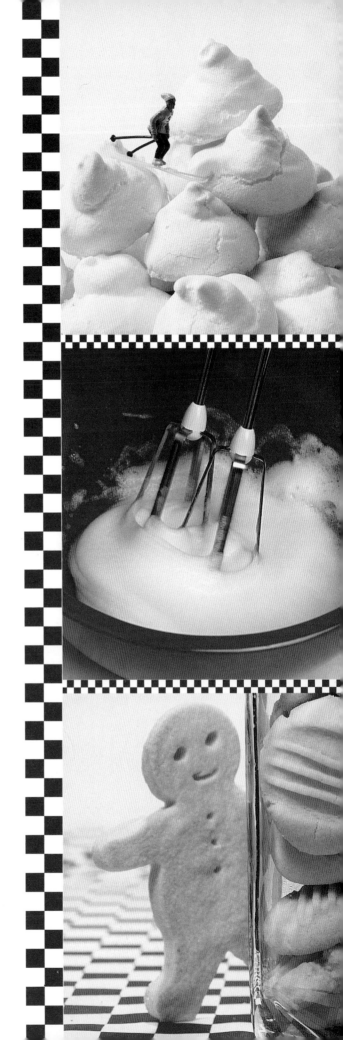

cherry pies or clever scones . . .

. . . then whisk up a mountain

Baking basics

Getting started
Here are the things you will need to bake the recipes in this book.

Weigh out your ingredients before you start, that way you won't leave anything out.

Warning!
Look out for this sign and take care.

Safe baking

• When you see this sign ask an adult to help you.
• An adult should always be around when you are in the kitchen.
• Ovens are HOT – wear your oven gloves.

weighing out

REMEMBER if you start a recipe using grams then stick to them. Don't mix up grams and ounces in one recipe.

MEASURING SPOONS – these are very useful, they have standard sizes from tablespoons to half teaspoons.

Kitchen rules

BE PREPARED – Lay out all the ingredients and utensils that you will need for the recipe.

CLEAN UP – always wash your hands before you cook.

COVER UP – Wear an apron to protect your clothes.

WASH & TIDY UP – It's your mess, you clear it up. Keep the kitchen tidy as you go along. Then you can cook again!

MEASURING JUG for measuring liquids.

WEIGHING SCALES for measuring dry ingredients.

MEASURING SPOONS for measuring small amounts e.g salt.

How long will it take?
The clock tells you how long to bake the recipe and will warn you to turn on the oven early to get it to the right temperature.

How much will it make?
This symbol tells you how much the recipe will make e.g 12 cookies or 24 mini breads.

4

your baking kit

WOODEN SPOON

COOKIE CUTTERS

PASTRY BRUSH

BAKING SHEET

SPOONS

FORK   KNIFE

LOAF TIN

ROLLING PIN

LOTS OF BOWLS

ELECTRIC WHISK

MUFFIN TIN

MIXING BOWL

BUN TIN

COOLING RACK

YOUR (CLEAN) HANDS

GREASEPROOF PAPER

CAKE TINS 18 CM (7 IN)

Cookie collection

To start you off

all you need are three things:

 +  +

Plain flour
150g (6 oz)

Caster sugar
50g (2 oz)

Butter
100g (4 oz)

= **24 cookies**
plain shortbread

Mmmm They look good!

1 recipe x 10

These aren't just ordinary cookies – with a little pinch here and a spot of decoration there, you can make 10 completely different cookies. 10 cookies in one!

1

2

3

4

5

6

7

8

9

yum yum

Turn the page
to discover the
magic ingredients.

10

7

How to make Shortbread cookies

Rubbing in – This is the way you mix the flour, butter, and sugar together. Rub the mixture between your thumb and fingertips until it looks like breadcrumbs (see page 46).

COOKIE EQUIPMENT

MIXING BOWL   BAKING TRAY   FORK   COOLING RACK

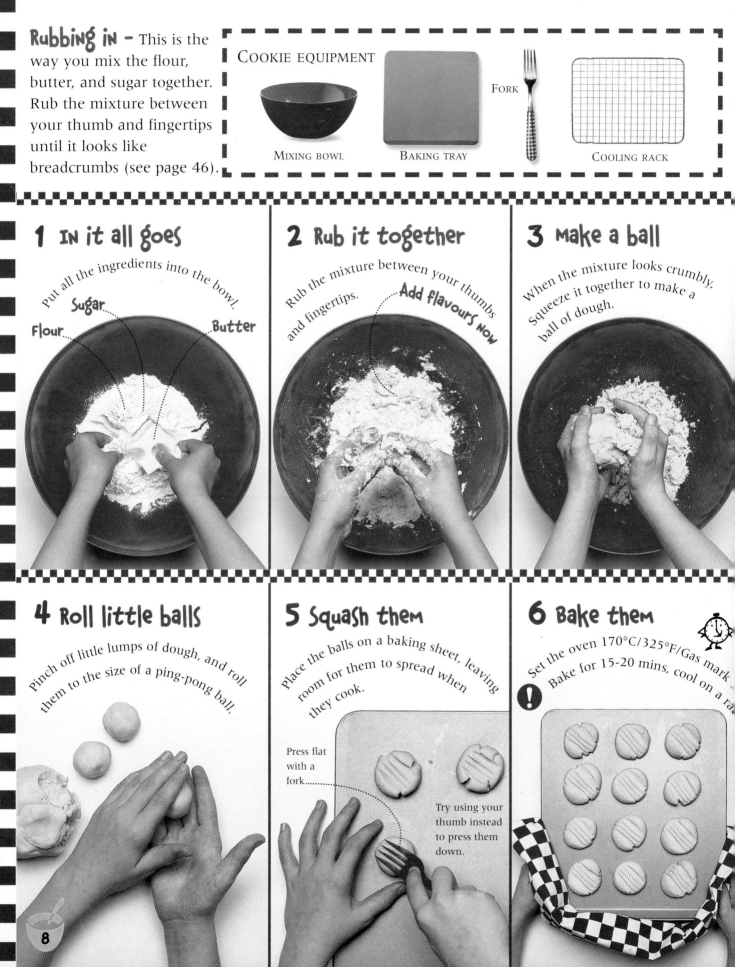

1 In it all goes
Put all the ingredients into the bowl.

Flour   Sugar   Butter

2 Rub it together
Rub the mixture between your thumbs and fingertips.

Add flavours now

3 Make a ball
When the mixture looks crumbly, squeeze it together to make a ball of dough.

4 Roll little balls
Pinch off little lumps of dough, and roll them to the size of a ping-pong ball.

5 Squash them
Place the balls on a baking sheet, leaving room for them to spread when they cook.

Press flat with a fork

Try using your thumb instead to press them down.

6 Bake them
Set the oven 170°C/325°F/Gas mark
Bake for 15-20 mins, cool on a ra

1 Chocolate chips
50g (2oz)

2 Cocoa powder
25g (1oz)

3 Coconut
50g (2oz)

4 Cinnamon
1 teaspoon

5 Sweeties
Press these into the cookies
before you bake them.

6 Peanut butter
1 tablespoon

Peanuts

7 Raisins
50g (2oz)

8 Almond essence
Add a few drops of almond essence
and stick an almond on the top.

9 Sugar strands
25g (1oz)

10 Chopped nuts
50g (2oz)

How to make 10 new cookies

Add your flavours at step 2.
If you want flavoured cookies, then add your cocoa, chocolate chips, coconut, or cinnamon at stage 2 when your mixture is crumbly. Decorate your cookies with the nuts or sweets just before you bake them.

Now get creative with your cookie cutters, see over the page.

create and bake

Bake me!

Make more of your cookie dough –
roll it out, cut out some shapes, then have
fun with icing.

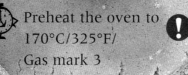

cookie dough
See page 8

Makes about
24 cookies

1. Roll out the dough

Sprinkle flour on your work surface and
a rolling pin. Now roll out
your dough until
it's 5 mm (¼ in)
thick, then choose
your cookie
cutters and get
shaping!

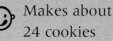

2. Ready to bake

Grease a baking tray (see page 46)
and place your shapes on
it, leaving spaces
between them.

Bake
for
15
minutes

Preheat the oven to
170°C/325°F/
Gas mark 3

3. Cool off

Carefully remove the tray from
the oven, let them cool a little on the
tray, then transfer to a cooling rack.

Tip – If it is difficult to roll, cut
the ball of dough in half, and roll out
one half at a time.

Ice and sprinkle

Icing – Mix up some icing sugar and water with drops of food colouring.

Icing Sugar
3 tablespoons

water
3 teaspoons

Food colouring

Now add some sprinkles.

Icing mix

Put 3 tablespoons of icing sugar in a bowl, add 3 teaspoons of water, and stir it in. Add more water if the icing is too thick.

Spoon the icing over the cookies and decorate them.

Adding colour

Use a cocktail stick to add colour to the icing mix. Keep adding and stirring until it's the colour you want.

Make holes with the end of a straw. Do this before you bake the cookie.

Use a cocktail stick to make smaller features like eyes.

Cut out a shape, then use a smaller cutter to make a new shape.

Cherry pies

Fill buttery pastry pies

with sweet fillings and feed them to your sweetheart.

Tinned cherry pie filling

Pastry
From page 14

+

Pie filling
200g (8oz) can

=

x 12 pies

Fruity pie fillings

When it's late summer get out and pick your own fresh fruit. Soft fruits, such as blackberries, are perfect and mix well with apple. Alternatively you can buy canned pie filling or try some of these other yummy ideas.

Makes 12 pies

Serve up your pies with a dusting of icing sugar and spoonful of custard

All kinds of pies

Apple pie

Peel and chop some eating apples and put them into a saucepan with a little sugar and a couple of tablespoons of water. Boil them until they are soft and when the mixture is cool, spoon it into pastry cases.

Mince pie

Just right for Christmas – a jar of mince meat is packed full of sultanas, peel, and raisins. Simply pop it in the pastry case.

Lemon curd pie

For a tangy taste, buy a jar of lemon curd. Spoon it straight into the cases and pop on the lid.

Red berry jam pie

Sweet strawberry or raspberry jam makes a perfect partner for the plain pastry case.

Marmalade pie

For a rich, zesty taste try using orange marmalade with thick peel.

Rub in and roll out

The pies are made with shortcrust pastry – it's handy for all sorts of recipes like sweet pies and tarts, and savouries, such as sausage rolls and egg flans.

Butter
125g (4oz)

+

Plain flour
250g (8oz)

+

water
4–8 teaspoons

=

Pastry
Makes about
12 pies

Rub the butter and flour together

1

2 Add some water.

3 Squeeze into a ball.

Make some pies

Make the leftovers into a ball and roll it out again.

Use the large cutter and press down firmly.

Don't press too hard. Add more flour if needed.

1 Roll out

Flour the surface and the rolling pin. Roll evenly over the pastry until it's about 5 mm (¼ inch) thick.

2 Make the pies

Gently place the pastry into the tin and fill the case with a spoonful or two of filling. Roll out more pastry and cut out the lids.

Roll out more pastry for the lid.

Gently rest the lid on top.

Don't over fill the cases, or they will overflow when cooked.

Use a straw to make a hole.

3 Ready to bake

Bake the pies. When they are ready let them cool in the tray then remove them and place on a rack.

Let them cool down before you take them out.

Leave to cool on a rack then serve up.

Preheat the oven to 170°C/325°F/ Gas mark 3

Bake for 15 minutes

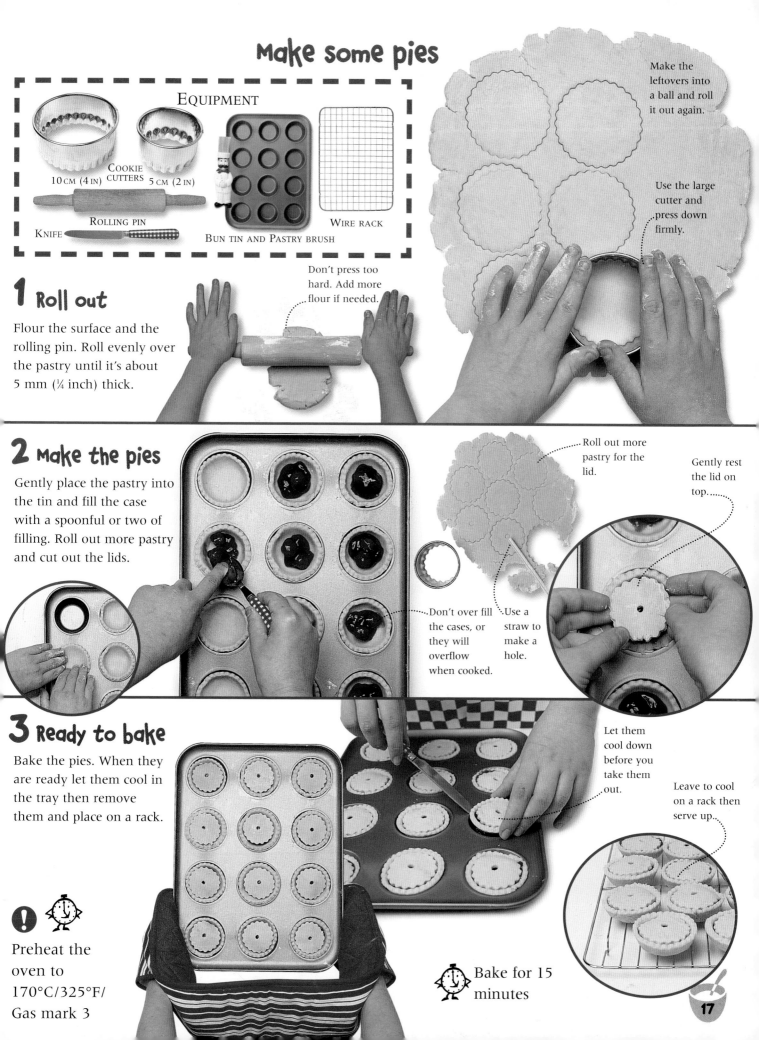

Tweetie pies

Crunchy nuts and seeds aren't just for birds – they make tasty nibbles to snack on anytime, even breakfast!

You will need

Butter
150g (6oz)

Soft brown sugar
100g (4oz)

Porridge oats
225g (8oz)

Honey
2 tablespoons

18

Now go nuts!

Add one of these **or** why not add them all?

Sultanas

Sesame seeds

Peanuts

Try 2 tablespoons
of each nut, seed, or fruit

Pumpkin
seeds

Sunflower
seeds

Pine nuts

Coconut

Chopped
nuts

☺ makes 18 pies

Mix up Some Pies

Crunchy pies – The longer you bake them, the crunchier they will get, and each bite will contain a completely different crunch!

Preheat the oven to 190°C/375°F/Gas mark 5 ❗

TWEETY PIE TOOLS

MIXING BOWL

WOODEN SPOON

KNIFE

DESSERT SPOON

PASTRY BRUSH

BUN TIN

COOLING RACK

20

Mix the butter and sugar together with a wooden spoon until the mixture is creamy.

Butter

Sugar

1 Cream together

Give it a stir.

2 Tip in the oats

Spoon up some mixture and roll it in a ball.

5 Make the pies

Grease the tin, then put in the ball of mixture.

6 Press them down

Then give it another stir.

Add as many as you like and stir them in.

3 Pour in the honey

4 Go nuts!

Bake in the oven for 10 to 15 minutes.

Use a knife to lift them out of the tray.

They will keep in an air-tight tin for two to three weeks.

7 Into the oven ❶

8 Leave to cool

Come for tea!

Fruit
Any dried fruit can be used. These are raisin scones spread with butter.

Sweet
Try these sweet scones with jam and cream.

Cheesy
These savoury scones are topped with grated cheese for an even tastier treat.

It's teatime!

Scones for tea - invite your friends round for sweet and savoury treats.

Butter
50g (2oz)

+

Self-raising flour
225g (8oz)

+

Milk
120ml (4fl oz)

=

1 plain scone

Makes 8 slices

Clever scones

Use this plain scone mixture to create new recipes. Just add all sorts of ingredients from sugar, dried fruit, and seeds to olives and cheese. Make a meal of them!

More tea Owl?
Have a scone with it.

Top row

Butter ⋯ **Flour** ⋯

Rub the butter and flour together to make breadcrumbs (see page 46).

1 Rub together

Add the sugar OR fruit OR cheese at this stage.

Mix the flavour in.

2 Add the flavours

3 Pour in the milk

Scones x 3

Make sweet or savoury – Follow the steps the same way for all the recipes. But at step 2 choose the flavour you want and mix it in. Then bake and enjoy them fresh from the oven.

Plain Sweet

25g (1 oz) Caster sugar

EQUIPMENT

BAKING TRAY

COOLING RACK

MIXING BOWL

PASTRY BRUSH   KNIFE

Bottom row

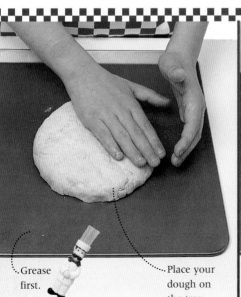

Grease first.

Place your dough on the tray.

7 put on a tray

Divide the dough up, 8 pieces works best.

8 Cut into sections

Brush with milk for a glossy finish.

9 Get ready to bake

Use a knife to stir the mixture.

4 Stir with a knife

Bring all the mixture together.

5 Make a ball

Flour a clean surface.

Flatten the ball to about 3 cm (1 in) thick.

Don't handle the dough too much.

6 Flour and flatten

Fruity

25g (1 oz) Caster sugar

125g (4 oz) raisins

Ultra Cheesy

75g (3 oz) Grated Cheddar cheese.

Sprinkle some of the cheese on top before you cook it.

Preheat the oven to 220°C/425°/ Gas mark 7.

Bake for 25 minutes, take out of the oven, and cool on a rack.

Scone tip
Eat it on the same day as you bake it.

I like to eat it fresh from the oven.

10 All done

Monkey bread

Bakes like a cake

and slices like bread.
Monkey enjoys a piece
for tea or a snack in his
lunch box.

*You'll go bananas
over my yummy recipe!*

EQUIPMENT

BOWL

LOAF TIN

COOLING RACK

PASTRY BRUSH

FORK

SPOON

WOODEN SPOON

Rub the butter and flour together until they are like breadcrumbs (see page 46).

1 Rubbing in

Add in sugar and raisins and give it a stir.

2 Add sugar and raisins

Beat the eggs, spoon out the honey, and stir them in.

3 Add eggs and honey

In a small bowl mash the bananas with a fork.

4 Mashed bananas

5 Add the bananas

6 Give it a stir

Dip the brush in oil and brush over the tin.

7 Grease the tin

Set the oven 180°C/350°F/Gas mark 4. Bake for 1 hour.

8 Pour it in

Is it cooked? Turn to page 46 to find out how to test it.

9 Leave to cool

Turn out your bread

Slide the knife between the cake and the tin.

10 Slide round a knife

Let the cake slip out of the tin.

11 Flip over the tin

The cake will cut more easily when it's cold.

12 Nearly ready to eat!

I like mine spread with butter

Slice up the bread and serve it up

Mini monkey muffins

To make these **yummy** muffins, use the same mixture as the monkey bread but fill a muffin tin instead.

☺ Makes 12 mini breads

MUFFIN TIN AND PAPER CASES

Just use your monkey bread mixture

Try these bread variations instead of bananas...

apple and cinnamon

2 apples peeled and chopped.

125ml (5 fl oz) milk

1 teaspoon cinnamon

Bunny bites

Grated peel and juice of an orange

2 carrots peeled and grated.

1 teaspoon mixed spice

As in step 5 on the previous page.

🕐 Preheat the oven to 180°C/350°F/ Gas mark 4 ❗

1 Stir it up

Carefully spoon in the mixture.

2 Fill up the cases

🕐 Bake them for 15 minutes. ❗

3 Bake your breads

making variations

To make the variations go back to step 5 of monkey bread, then instead of adding the banana put in the ingredients for apple or carrot breads and mix it all up in the same way.

carrot bunny bites

Storage

Eat them warm or keep them fresh in an airtight tin. They'll keep for about two weeks.

Mini monkey muffins

Apple and cinnamon

Chocolate chunk cookies

Forget Shop-bought cookies, these are much tastier! Use a good quality chocolate chopped up into big chunks.

Makes 12 cookies

You will need . . .

Soft brown Sugar
70g (2½ oz)

Caster Sugar
70g (2½ oz)

Butter
125g (4½ oz)

1 Egg

Plain flour
175g (7 oz)

Bicarbonate of Soda
1 teaspoon

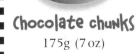

Chocolate chunks
175g (7 oz)

EQUIPMENT

MIXING BOWL

SPOON

KNIFE

WOODEN SPOON

BAKING TRAY

PASTRY BRUSH

COOLING RACK

1 Start creaming

Butter

Brown and caster Sugar

Soft butter is easier to mix with the sugar.

2 Add beaten egg

See page 47 to beat an egg.

Preheat the oven to 190°C/375°F/Gas mark 5

3 Stir in the flour

Mix in the flour.

4 Add choc chunks

Get help to chop the chunks.

5 Spoon onto tray

Spoon four heaps on each tray.

6 Bake them

Bake for 10–12 minutes then take out of the oven and cool on a rack.

7 Cooling down

Prepare the tray for the next batch of cookies.

Let them cool before moving to a rack.

Eat them when they are still warm

Choc tip
Stick chunks of chocolate on top of the heaps before cooking.

Happy birthday Bear!
Let's have a party,
we can ask Owl to come.

Yes please!

Bake a cake

...and celebrate with this chocolate-covered treat. Share it with your special friends when you have a reason to say...

"Let's have a party!"

Mmm chocolate

Makes 8–12 slices

How's your cake Little Ted?

All-in-one mix

Simply beat all the ingredients together in the bowl.

This recipe makes a plain sponge cake. Baking two cakes means you can layer them up and fill it with jam or fresh cream. You can also add flavour to the mixture like cocoa powder, dried fruit, or vanilla.

Baking powder
1 teaspoon

Flour
125g (4oz)
Self raising flour

Eggs
2 large

Butter
125g (4oz)
Softened butter

Sugar
125g (4oz)
Caster sugar

Bake a cake

Sponge cake

Divide the mixture evenly between two lined tins (see page 47). Spread the mixture flat so the cake rises evenly. Let them cool down before you spread on the topping. Keep the cake in a cool place and eat within two days.

Preheat the oven to 170°C/325°F/ Gas mark 3

Top and fill

Chocolate cream

Use good quality chocolate mixed with double cream. Melt the chocolate first then spoon in the cream.

Chocolate
200g (7oz)

Double cream
6 tablespoons

1 Fill the tins

Prepare the tins (see page 47).

Share the mixture between the tins.

2 Spread the mixture

Spread the mixture out to the sides evenly.

Bake in the oven for 20 minutes

1 Melt the chocolate

Stir the chunks around to help them melt.

Take care, HOT water.

2 Add the cream

Take the bowl away from the hot water.

Stir the cream into the melted chocolate.

make the mixture

Put all the ingredients into a bowl and whisk together for two minutes. Keep the whisk on a low setting.

EQUIPMENT

MIXING BOWL

ELECTRIC WHISK

KNIFE

SPOON

WIRE RACK

2 CAKE TINS 18 CM (7 IN)

PASTRY BRUSH

GREASEPROOF PAPER

Melting choc

To melt the chocolate, pour very hot water into a bowl. Sit another bowl on top and pop the chocolate in. The heat from the water will melt it.

Break the chocolate into chunks first.

Very hot water – don't over fill the bowl.

Take care – HOT water

Run a knife around the edge where the cake may stick to the tin.

Allow the cakes to cool down.

3 Out of the oven

Hold the rim of the tin.

Give it a bit of a tap.

Tip the cake out of the tin.

4 Remove the cakes

Carefully peel back the paper.

The cakes should be cold before the adding the topping.

5 Leave to get cold

Place the top layer on

Put two spoonfuls on the bottom layer.

Spread it over with a knife.

3 Spread the filling

Spoon on the rest of the mixture.

4 Pour on the topping

Use a knife to spread the mixture over the top and down the sides.

5 Spread it all over

meringue mountain

whisk up egg whites into sweet frothy peaks to make delicious desserts.

Egg whites
2 whites

+

Caster Sugar
125g (4oz)

=

Makes about
12 small peaks

See page 48 for how to separate an egg

Fruity nest

Spoon thick cream onto a nest and top it off with pieces of fruit.

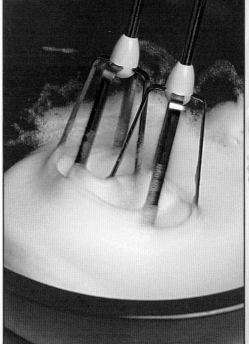

Peak sandwich

Sandwich two meringue peaks together with thick cream.

Mmmmeringue

Meringues are made from egg whites mixed with sugar baked in a very cool oven until they are crunchy on the outside and soft inside – mmmm!

Serve up your meringues with cream and fruit or just on their own.

It's ready when you can turn the bowl upside-down over your head without the egg whites sliding.

Use a big clean bowl.

See page 48 for how to separate the egg whites.

Use the whisk at top speed.

3 IS it ready?

1 whisk the egg whites

2 Keep whisking

whisk up a mountain

whisking is fun - An electric whisk makes the egg white froth up quicker than by hand, but remember to stop it spinning before you take it out of the bowl, or you'll cover the kitchen!

Meringue hints and tips

• Whisk the egg whites just enough – try the "over the head" test as in step 3.
• Add the sugar a tablespoon at a time while whisking. Keep repeating this until all the sugar is used up.
• Grease the tray first to stop the paper slipping.

Grease the tray then cover with greaseproof paper.

Preheat the oven to 140°C/275°F/ Gas mark 1

7 Spoon out some peaks

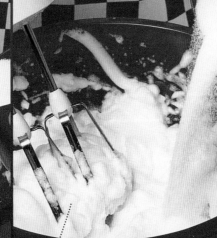

Pour in the sugar – about a tablespoon at a time.

Whisk in the sugar BUT not at full speed.

See page 46 for whisking tips.

When all the sugar is in give the mixture a final whisk.

The mixture should look glossy and stand up in peaks.

4 Add some sugar and whisk

5 Keep whisking

6 Now it's peaky

EQUIPMENT

MIXING BOWL

ELECTRIC WHISK

TEASPOON AND DESSERT SPOON

GREASEPROOF PAPER

BAKING SHEET

PASTRY BRUSH

Press the peak down with a spoon to make a nest.

Make a snowman with peaks joined together.

Bake in the oven for 2 hours.

8 Ready to bake

Take the meringues out of the oven.

Leave them for a few hours to dry out.

9 All dried out

Bits-in bread

Make bread taste more interesting by using grainy flour and sprinkles of seeds inside and out.

Bits-in bread is fun to bake and eat.

You will need:

Butter
25g (1 oz)

Bits-in Flour
225g (8 oz)
Strong granary
bread flour

white flour
225g (8 oz)
Strong white
bread flour

yeast
1 sachet
Fast-action yeast
(2 teaspoons)

Sugar and salt
1 teaspoon
Brown sugar,
1 teaspoon Salt

water
275ml (10 fl oz)
Warm water

And a beaten egg
for a glossy
finish

Makes 12
rolls

Bits-in and on bread. As well as adding some seeds to your bread mixture, sprinkle a few on top – not just for decoration but because they make the bread taste good too!

You will need lots of different seeds

Sesame seeds

Poppy seeds

Sunflower seeds

Pumpkin seeds

41

Make a dip to pour the water in.

Mix it with a wooden spoon.

Put the flour, yeast, sugar, and salt in a bowl and rub in the butter.

Add some seeds now if you want more bits.

Make it a ball with your hands.

1 Rub together

2 Add water

3 Mix it up

How to make bread

Bread flour – It's important to use special bread flour, called strong flour. It comes in white, wholemeal, and granary, and for this recipe it has malt grains in it too.

Bread tips

Yeast likes warmth to help it grow and this will help your bread to rise.

• If all the things you work with are warm, such as the bowl and the room, this will help.

• Make sure the water isn't too hot or this will kill the yeast and your bread won't rise.

A beaten egg

Grease the tray.

Place the dough balls on the tray.

Cover with clingfilm and leave in a warm place for about 40 minutes.

When they have doubled in size, they are ready to decorate.

Brush them with beaten egg.

7 Prepare the tray

8 The rolls have grown!

Sprinkle lots of flour on the surface.
Stretch the dough and fold it over. (See page 46.)

4 Knead the dough

Press your knuckles into the dough.
Add more flour if needed.
Repeat steps 4 and 5 for 6 minutes.

5 Keep kneading

Make into a ball and cut it into
12 even-sized pieces. Roll them into small balls.

6 Divide it up

Preheat the oven to
220°C/425°F/
Gas mark 7

EQUIPMENT

KNIFE

WOODEN SPOON

BAKING TRAY

PASTRY BRUSH

MIXING BOWL

CLINGFILM

COOLING RACK

Now sprinkle
on the seeds.

9 Get ready to bake

Bake for 20 to 25
minutes, then take
out of the oven and
cool on a rack.

Serve up your rolls
fresh from the oven
with you favourite filling

43

Mould your dough

Now it's time to play with your dough. Make a dough ball as shown before, but before you bake it try moulding it into different shapes.

Cooking the shapes

Follow the steps as for bits-in bread, place your shapes on a greased tin, cover them, and allow them to rise until they are twice the size. Then bake for 25 minutes.

Plaited bread

1 Roll your dough into three sausage shapes.

2 Squeeze your dough together at one end.

3 Bring one sausage over to the middle.

Repeat on the other side.

Carry on plaiting then squash the ends together and place on the tray.

Dough balls

Roll into a sausage shape, then cut and roll into dough balls.

or a Pizza

1 Flatten a dough ball.

Grated cheese

Chopped olives

Spread a tablespoon of tomato purée on first.

Then a tablespoon of chopped tinned tomato.

2 Add some toppings, then bake in the oven.

Dough boy

Make small balls of dough and stick them to your rolls to make faces.

44

Bread tastes best when it's warm from the oven.

Try serving dough balls with garlic butter.

Garlic butter

You can bake

Baking Methods

Baking recipes use different methods to mix the same ingredients to achieve different results. Whether it's biscuits, cakes, or pastry, this book uses a few of the basic methods. Here they are with explanations of what they do.

Rubbing in

Using your thumb and fingertips, rub the butter and flour together until the mixture looks like breadcrumbs. This is used for a lot of the recipes in this book such as pastry and cookies.

Creaming

This is when you mix or beat the butter and sugar together with a wooden spoon so that they make a creamy mixture. In this book it's used to start the chunky choc cookies.

Dough

Dough is a name given to the mixture that makes pastry, biscuits, scones, or bread, but they behave differently when they are cooked. Bread dough needs kneading as this has yeast in it. Other dough should be handled lightly.

Tips

Let your dough rest in the fridge for half an hour before using it.

To store your dough wrap it in plastic and put in the fridge.

Cookie and pastry dough

Kneading

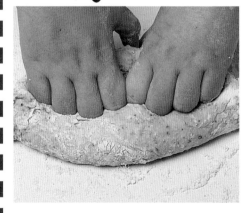

This is what you do to bread dough to get the yeast working. Fold the dough over itself and press your knuckles into it. Repeat this over and over again. Then leave it in a warm place to rise.

Whisking

Whisking egg whites can be done with a hand whisk but an electric one is much faster. Don't let any egg yolk in or it won't work. Whisk at full speed until the mixture stands up in peaks.

Is it cooked?

To check if the monkey bread is cooked, put a skewer in the centre of it when it's due to come out of the oven. If the skewer comes out with some mixture on it, it's not cooked so put it back in the oven.

To keep your cookies, cakes, and tweety pies fresh, store them in an AIRTIGHT tin and they will keep f a week or two.

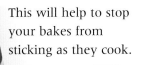

Greasing baking tins

This will help to stop your bakes from sticking as they cook.

Put a little oil onto a pastry brush and sweep it all over the tin.

Oil

Line a tin with paper

To make sure your bakes have no chance of sticking, line the tin with greaseproof paper. Brush the tin with oil first so that the paper sticks to it.

Use the paper to pull the cake out of the tin when the cake is cooked.

1 Draw around the base of the tin.

Greaseproof paper

2 Cut out the shape.

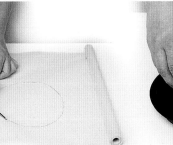

3 Place the paper in the tin.

Grease the tin first.

Crack open an egg

How to get an egg out of the shell.

The secret is to be firm and gentle at the same time.

tap tap

1 Tap the egg firmly against the edge of a bowl.

2 Gently press your thumbs into the crack.

3 Pull the two shells apart and let the egg fall out.

white

yellow yolk

Beating an egg

Mixing the egg white and yolk together.

It's best to beat an egg before adding it to a recipe.

Use a fork to mix.

Move it quickly in a circular action.

Separate an egg – the easy way

Sometimes you will only want the egg white or the yolk. So you need to separate them carefully. It takes a bit of practice so have some spare eggs in case you break the yolk.

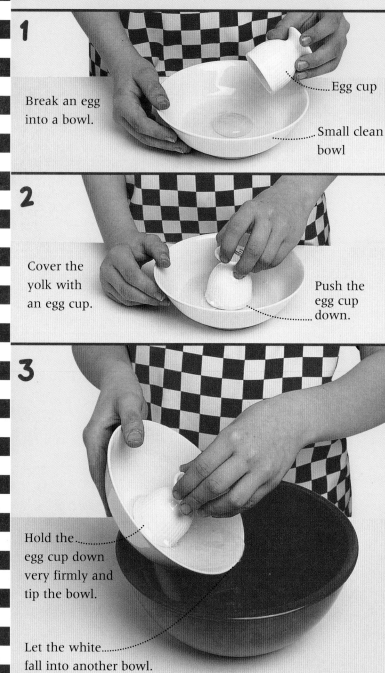

1 Break an egg into a bowl.

Egg cup

Small clean bowl

2 Cover the yolk with an egg cup.

Push the egg cup down.

3 Hold the egg cup down very firmly and tip the bowl.

Let the white fall into another bowl.

Meringue tip
Don't get any egg yolk in the egg white or your meringues won't work.

Put the yolk in another bowl.

Acknowledgements

With thanks to...
Billy Bull, James Bull, Seriya Ezigwe, Daniel Ceccarelli, Harry Holmstoel for being keen chefs.

All images © Dorling Kindersley.
For further information see:
www.dkimages.com